ADVANCEMENT OF LEARNING

The
Advancement of Learning
(1649)

BY

JOHN HALL

EDITED BY

A. K. CROSTON

LIVERPOOL
at the University Press
1953

LIVERPOOL REPRINTS
NUMBER 7

GENERAL EDITOR
L. C. MARTIN

PRINTED BY JOHN BELLOWS LIMITED
GLOUCESTER

INTRODUCTION

JOHN HALL of Durham (1627–56) is still remembered as a minor poet of the seventeenth century: his *Poems* were reprinted by Brydges in 1816 and again in 1906 in Saintsbury's *Minor Poets of the Caroline Period*, ii. But Hall is of interest on other counts; he was indeed a most versatile writer, and many seventeenth-century literary forms are represented in his works.

He was born in Durham in August 1627 of 'gentilitial' parents (Brydges).[1] His going up to Cambridge was delayed by the outbreak of the Civil War. He seems to have studied assiduously at home—'improved himself to a miracle' (Wood); and when he eventually went up to St. John's College in February 1645/6 he soon made a name for himself. His essays, written in the Baconian manner, were published in 1646 under the title *Horae Vacivae* and prefaced by many commendatory poems. These essays, according to Davies, ' amazed not onely the University, but the more

[1] Hall appears in the *D.N.B.* His friend John Davies of Kidwelly gives a biography in his edition of Hall's translation of *Hierocles upon the Golden Verses of Pythagoras* (1657). Other details of his life will be found in Wood, *Athenae Oxonienses*, ii, 460 (ed. Bliss, 1815) and in an article by P. S. Havens, ' A tract long attributed to Milton', *The Huntington Library Bulletin*, November 1934, pp. 109–14. Brydges' brief account in the introduction to his edition of the poems is derived from Wood. The *Humble Motion* is discussed by J. B. Mullinger in *The University of Cambridge* (1911), iii, pp. 371–5 ; the most detailed account is in R. F. Jones's *Ancients and Moderns* (1936), pp. 100–3.

serious part of men in the three Nations'.[1] They
appear to have been well received also on the continent
and were translated into French. The *Poems* appeared
in the following January (1646/7). But in May, having
failed to get a fellowship, Hall went down from
Cambridge and entered Gray's Inn.[2] Between May
and August he married a gentlewoman of Hertfordshire,
carrying her off against many suitors. The marriage
was not successful: a feud between the two families
and discontent between the couple themselves made
the lady 'in a manner a widdow soon after the
Nuptials'. George Wharton (see below) gives a more
biased account: Hall betrayed the 'comely Maid',

> And when had done with her (*Poor soul*) He sent her
> Home to her *Father* to supply her *renter*.

His poverty forced him to undertake political
journalism; he alternated for the rest of his short life
between 'cultural' publications and pamphleteering.

In 1647 he edited Robert Hegge's *In Aliquot Sacrae
Paginae loca Lectiones* and wrote *A True Account and
Character of the Times*—signing the latter pamphlet
'N.LL.' He seems also to have tried his hand at a
romance. This was unfortunately never returned by a
friend to whom it was lent. It might, says Davies,
'have raised envie in the famous Romancist Mounsieur
De Scudary'. Also in 1647 he seems to have published
translations from Andreae, *Model of Christian Society
and the Right hand of Christian love offered*, these

[1] 'An account of the Author', prefixed to *Hierocles*.
Quotations given below without reference are from this
biography.
[2] Davies says that he entered his name at Gray's Inn a year
before going to London.

probably being reprinted as additions to the posthumous work *Of the advantageous reading of History* (1657).[1] In 1648 Hall was employed by Lilly, the astrologer, to run a government paper, *Mercurius Britannicus*, which was directed against the royalist paper, *Mercurius Elenctitus*, of Lilly's rival-astrologer, Captain George Wharton. During 1648 Hall published a volume of *Emblems with Elegant Figures* and, according to Davies, a *Satire against Presbytery* which does not seem to have survived. About this time he left Gray's Inn, or so Wharton asserts in a series of attacks on Hall. Wharton calls Hall the ' *Grayes-Inne* Wild-Goose ' in No. 28 of *Mercurius Elenctitus* (31 May–7 June); in No. 29 (7–14 June) he asserts that Hall's recompense from Lilly ' wil scarce mend *his Bootes* '; and in No. 34 (12–19 July) he claims to have ' *unkennelled* that *Vermine*, and made him shift his *Quarters* from *Grayes-Inne* ': Hall now ' *lurkes* in the *Adulterous Lapps of his Bloomsbury-beauties*'. Wharton is of course hardly reliable, and the scurrilous verses which he writes against Hall need not be taken very seriously. Hall's poverty at any rate seemed in way of amendment in 1649 when he became an official government pamphleteer at £100 a year.[2]

The only published work to be discovered in 1649 is the pamphlet here reprinted; it may be said to

---

[1] See G. H. Turnbull, *Hartlib, Dury and Comenius* (1947), especially p. 74, n. 4.

[2] *C.S.P.D.*, 1649–50, p. 139 (14 May 1649) ; qu. Havens, op. cit., p. 111. Havens gives all the relevant quotations for Hall from *C.S.P.D.*

combine successfully both Hall's 'cultural' and 'official' interests.[1]

In the following year Hall was commissioned to go as observer for the official paper *Mercurius Politicus* with Cromwell on his invasion of Scotland. Hall assisted Marchamont Nedham in the conducting of this paper until 1653 (under the supervision of Milton from 1651). During 1650 Hall published under the name 'J. de la Salle', a rather schoolboyish pseudonym he sometimes used, his *Paradoxes*, re-issuing them in an enlarged form in 1653. Also in 1650 he was called to the Bar, but the remaining years of his life seem for the most part to have been lean and wretched. His writings at this time need not all be mentioned here. During his Scottish trip he wrote *The Grounds and Reasons of Monarchy Considered*, which ran to three editions during 1650 and 1651. In the latter year he republished the 'Amboyna tracts' of 1624 and 1632 in a successful attempt to frustrate, by reviving old atrocity stories, the treaty-seeking efforts of the Dutch. In 1652 he published *Dionysius Longinus of the Height of Eloquence*, the first English translation—' a piece very elaborate, and accordingly much esteemed in both Universities'. In 1653 appeared the tract, *A Letter Written to a Gentleman in the Country*, which was formerly attributed to Milton.[2] In 1654 appeared Hall's translation of the *Lusus serius* of Michael Maierus.

The payment of Hall's pension was irregular, and although this may not have unduly perturbed him—

---

[1] Although it was perhaps printed before the granting of the pension. See note to **13.** 13–14.

[2] The correct attribution is demonstrated in Havens, op. cit.

Davies observes that ' the very want of money could never raise in him any esteem of it, sildom receiving or paying any himself '—his life became increasingly purposeless. His health deteriorated so much that he lost the power to satisfy the government at all, and in 1655 (17 April) his pension was officially cancelled. After Easter he went to St. Albans in an attempt to regain his health ; there he translated Hierocles ; but his health did not improve. On hearing of his father's fatal illness he managed to travel north to Durham—to die there himself on 1 August 1656. At the time of his death he was engaged on a translation of Procopius's *Anecdota* (Davies).

Davies gives us several examples of Hall's energy: of the *Lusus serius* he says : ' Almost one half of it was done in one afternoon, over a glasse of wine in a Tavern '; and the *Humble Motion* was ' written in four mornings '. Hall's memory was vast—and he was ' universally read '. He could dictate four or five hours together. In other respects he was rather casual: he looked on a barber as a ' tedious torment '; and when threatened with fatness, rather than take exercise he swallowed pebbles. He seems to have had many acquaintances. At Cambridge these included Henry More, and he corresponded with Hartlib. His London, acquaintances included Hobbes who said of him that

> Had not his debauches & intemperance diverted him from the more serious studies, he had made an extraordinary person ; for no man had ever done so great things at his age.[1]

Hall's *Humble Motion* is in several ways a representative mid-seventeenth-century document, showing

[1] Davies, quoted by Wood, ed. cit., ii, 460.

how alive its author was to the contemporary ' climate of opinion '.

Bacon is the major influence, as is suggested by the full title; and, like Bacon, Hall devotes the preliminary space of his *Advancement of Learning* to defence. His main contribution, however, is an intensified exultation in the prospects of the New Age, and the whole pamphlet is dominated and warmed by this visionary excitement. For Hall, ' knowledge hath no limits '; the age is opening to a boundless future; and if the Parliament seizes its chance it will ' command abundance of fruitfull wits which shall every day bud forth with some invention, serviceable either to the necessities of the poor, or graver magnificence of the rich '. The utilitarian note is strong in Hall as in the later disciples of Bacon. An all-powerful science will give endless blessings to man provided he pursues the ' gallantest theories of knowledge'. The vision, moreover, is close to realization: ' he is not acquainted with the Business of knowledge that knows not what sensible increases (I had almost said perfection) it hath of late arrived to '.

Hall is also in the Bacon tradition in what he has to say about the ' mists of ignorance and superstition ' of past ages. And his constant stress on ' particulars ' and ' things ' is obviously to be related to Bacon's objections to the verbalism of medieval philosophy. Hall demands particularity in several divisions of learning: and in his search for the key-science he rejects metaphysics because it is ' abstrusely abstract'. The widespread seventeenth-century opposition of *words* and *things*, perhaps the most persistent idea which passed from Bacon to the champions of the Royal Society, inevitably appears in Hall; and it goes with the emphasis on ' real ' knowledge, which will fill men's minds with ' delicate ravishing contemplations '.

An almost ecstatic belief in the possibilities of scientific progress and a dislike for traditional learning are, then, the chief qualities of Hall's pamphlet, and they clearly derive from Bacon. Details of thought and expression in which Hall echoes Bacon are pointed out in the notes to this reprint.

Much of the distrust of conventional learning is to be found also, of course, in Descartes, by whom it is presented in the same personal way it is here. Hall comes close to Descartes in the use of an autobiographical preliminary to his discussion of method, and also in his conclusion that the first necessity of learning is ' doubtfulnesse ': a scepticism to be brought to bear upon anything ' which was not fortified with strong reason and right experience '.

The third writer to be mentioned as having influenced Hall is Milton. One or two phrases in the *Humble Motion* may possibly be derived from the *Areopagitica*, including perhaps the word 'Areopagitick' itself. And as J. B. Mullinger notes,[1] several of the points in Hall on current teaching of Latin and Greek, logic, metaphysics, and ethics are closely paralleled in Milton's *Of Education*, which Hall admired.[2] There is, however, a difference of tone and emphasis between Milton and Hall. For Milton the primary object of

[1] Op. cit., pp. 372–3.
[2] Hall wrote to Hartlib (21 December ? 1644) : ' I am much ambitious of the acquaintance of Mr. Milton (who is here said to be the author of that excellent discourse of education you were pleased to impart)' (qu. G. H. Turnbull, op. cit., p. 39).

learning is religious : ' to repair the ruins of our first
parents by regaining to know God aright'. Hall, it is
true, puts religion at the forefront of his programme,
but he also, as has been mentioned, gives a very
prominent place to sceptical reason, which he favours
not only in secular studies : the ' sublime understandings ' are those that call all things to the ' Test of
reason ' and demand ' forcible demonstrations and
porismaticall inferences of nature ' such as may ' not
precariously, but irresistably infer a Deity '. And
whereas for Milton ' truth ' lies in the knowledge of a
personal God, whom we are to love and imitate, Hall
conceives of an ' abstract wisdom ' desiring man to find
the truth through the ' paths and Mazes of Science '.

Hall's utilitarian outlook serves further to distinguish him from Milton, whose secondary aim in
education is to fit a man ' to perform justly, skilfully,
and magnanimously all the offices both private and
public of peace and war.' The ideal of manhood recom-
mended here is, as Dr Tillyard observes,[1] the many-
sided one of the Renaissance. Hall thinks rather of
the ' facilitation of business ' in various specialized
fields, suggesting, for instance, the compilation of
topographical and political accounts of various states,
the publication of Natural History digests (fore-
shadowing the *Philosophical Transactions* of the Royal
Society); and together with demonstrations of Botany
and Mathematics and lectures on antiquities, new chairs
are clearly demanded in Chemistry and Anatomy.
Education is to be suited to the capacity of the
student—whose natural bent is to be studied in infancy
and later education adapted to the job he is most fitted

[1] *Milton* (1930), p. 153.

to perform, whether ' ignoble ' or ' worthy '. Hall, in
fact, looks forward to the scientifically planned state.

There is nevertheless a link with Milton in Hall's
demand for the repeal of ' that hatefull gagg of
licensing'. The defence of learning in the middle of the
seventeenth century, although it could rely on power-
ful advocates and could appeal to strong emotional
forces, was still very necessary.[1]   Hall's pamphlet
comes just before the main Puritan attacks on the
universities had developed.[2] But the argument that
direct study of the word of God was all that was
necessary for salvation was already formidable—more
so than in the days of Cornelius Agrippa or of Bacon.
Hall, like Milton, defends learning from within the
Puritan ranks. He echoes Milton's appeal for liberty,
an appeal that runs through the writings of the saner
seventeenth-century attempts to reform education
whether these refer to an older ideal like Milton's or
aim at establishing the new science on a firm basis.

One or two minor points may be mentioned. Hall
shows that concern for national prestige which we find
in Milton and equally in the more partisan Moderns :
the luring of foreign students to England is a strong
point in Hall's appeal to Parliament. We may also
note the hostility to pulpit eloquence: traditional
learning serves only for ' idle Priests, to make their
sermons more gaudy ', a theme to be developed later

[1] See, for instance, the preface to Richard Whitlock's
Zootomia (1654), reprinted in this present series (1949).

[2] See R. F. Jones (op. cit., ch. V), who refers particularly
to Wood, History and Antiquities of the University of Oxford
(1796), pp. 657, 680, 683, 696–7.

in the century into a full scale attack on pulpit eloquence.[1]

But the point to stress in conclusion is Hall's radiant vision of progress. Bacon, in his *De Interpretatione Naturae Proœmium*, forecasts the civil wars and sees in them a storm ' fatal for literature and science '.[2] Hall, writing when the wars are over, sees the time as ripe for all glory; and in the insistent rhythms with which he ends his pamphlet he looks forward to the great rewards when Religion is purged of superstition, when Nature is forced into ' open veracity and pure nakedness ', when Arts multiply, when ' easie and naturall ' political orders are evolved, when the ' wayes of Education are made smooth', and when posterity shall possess ' all the Treasures of reall knowledge '.

---

[1] See R. F. Jones, ' The Attack on Pulpit Eloquence in the Restoration ', *J.E.G.P.*, xxx (1931).

[2] Bacon, *Works*, ed. Spedding, Ellis and Heath, iii, 519.

An
Humble Motion
To
The PARLIAMENT
Of
ENGLAND

Concerning
The ADVANCEMENT
of *Learning*:
And
Reformation of the Universities.

By J. H.

LONDON,

Printed for *John Walker*, at the Starre
in *Popes-Head-Alley*. *MDC IL.*

TO THE

PARLIAMENT.

I T hath been the usuall method of that E-
ternall Wisdome in the pursuance of any
of his high Designes, to render his Instruments, while they continued faithfully use-
full, full of honour and successe : But when
they once began either to stand still, or look back ; to de-
cline that honour which he had formerly cast upon
them, and to wrap it up in a cloud of forgetfulnesse   10
and misery ; and then raise up such other means, which
though to the eye of Reason they might appeare con-
temptible, should carry on his great worke to a just period, and make a full assertion of his glory, in despite of
all the wicked cunning and resolution of men and the
deepest Theorems of contrary policy.

That

That this Assertion is neither vain nor new, I need not
call in the Aids of any remoter Histories, if I appeale
from the walls where you now sit in counsell, to the
eyes wherewith you now see, you will finde as strange
and as noble an assertion of this Thesis, as was ever be-
held by any Age or Nation. For whereas at first you
met together by the conduct of a strong Providence (which in spight of all opposition and backward-
nesse of these times and powers assembled you together) and begun more seriously and couragiously to   10
weigh what a heavy trust lay upon your shoulders; such
of you who were early labourers, cannot but with joy
remember through what pangs and throws you were
delivered of the first attempt of Freedome ; when that
great Bugbear of a continuall and shining power (which
though it endeavoured to seem a great light of it selfe,
yet was onely an opake dense body, and had no other
splendour but the reflection of yours) hung back, nay
was possessed against you, when some ill-beholden to
their education had not shaken off those prejudices   20
which commonly attend men that judge according to
their first thoughts; and others who could not but make
a right judgement of things, being either byassed by interest, or poysoned with hopes, grew cold toward you ;
what a labour was it to make one head, (which had it
followed the Law, might have as much obliged the Nation as any whatsoever) an oblation to a betrayed and
oppressed people ? Nay when that was done, and an
Army not of our owne Nation, with excessive care and
charge removed; how were you encumbred by a violent   30
and sturdy humour, which would not suffer you to make
use of those little advantages of liberty which you had
al-

already gained, but assayed to returne you under the former, if not a severer Tyranny.

But the counsels of men were abortive, and you were reserved for greater matters, that humour burst forth like an Impostume, and went out from you, which had it continued within, and not professed open hostility, had been dangerous, if not fatall. But when you were once left to your selves, you had power to act more vigorously, and by a happy *Antiperistasis* to grow more intense ; so being closely united in the Centre, you 10 bravely brake through that stiffe circumference that beset you, and were made the Masters of many happy and signall Victories.

Yet those Victories seemed notwithstanding to carry a fate with them; for whereas your excessive lenity had permitted some of your conquered enemies to lodge a-midst you, they scattered such a quicke and powerfull contagion among those whom you represent, and especially the chiefe City, that there were apparent symptomes of a relapse, which was shortly followed by such 20 a dangerous sicknesse, that if you had not been miraculously aided with an almost immediate hand of Providence, you had never overcome, and yet you suddenly, and ere your selves could imagine, wrastled out of it.

But when your Victories were redoubled with these successes, there wanted not some who sate in counsell among you, who to say no worse, either durst not, or would not be couragious in following those opportunities wherewith Providence courted you ; nay they so retarded you by cunning crosse debates, that your 30 latter peace seemed far more dangerous to you, then either of your former wars, you standing strugling with
this

this oppressive humour, and not discovering any signs of motion, unlesse it were of Retrogradation ; whilst you enabled your conquered enemy to give you what was already yours, and stroke you with such concessions, as you had far more reason to dread, then any of his former Proclamations or menaces.

But how soon were all these corrupt counsellours purged from among you, and dis-inabled for to disperse any of their infection ? whilst you being loosed from those charms wherewith you before were *maleficiate*, 10 began to act powerfully and smartly, and indeed performed more in a few months, then you had done before in twice as many yeares, or your Ancestours could doe in the double number of Centuries.

I mention this with no other designe, then for your glory (for you have cleared our liberties, and set them now on the right Base, having by a transcendent comprehensive peece of Justice, removed the common oppressour) and also to tell you, that unlesse you doe not 20 also not rest here, but even run forward to the end of that course to which the divine will shall by apparent signes direct you, the worke will be taken out of your hands and put into others, who finishing it with the life and constancy which you ought to have done, must expect that reward and honour which waited on you.

I say not thus much that either I feare it in you, or that I can gather any even remote causes of feare, but that I would from it say, that unlesse you doe absolutely alter the complexion and temper of the Commonwealth, and endeavour to your utmost to provide the 30 best means to preserve it in the best constitution for the future; all that which you have hitherto done for us, will prove nothing, if not evill.   Now

Now by what means this may be effected, I have neither vanity nor impudence enough to direct you, especially since you seem to the exactest judgement of man,
to be as happy in re-erecting, as you were fortunate in
pulling down, and to take such a course both in matters
Divine, Civill, and Military, as may, as much as possible
stifle or render abortive all the machinations of future
mischiefe, and avoid those errours and imperfections
which cannot be exempted from humane Lawes. But
yet (as here you must bee acknowledged for res-   10
cuing that liberty which warrants this freedome) all
these cares, which are so pious, so noble, so worthy of
such Lawgivers, will be found neither intense nor large
enough, if ye remit one grand consideration which must
diffuse it selfe through all, and knit them together;
nay bestow on them both form and vigour: The most
effectuall advancement, I meane, not the bare permissive
propagation of Learning.

Somewhat you have done in this kinde, but how
much to this purpose I cannot judge; for besides that it   20
reached no further then Politicall aimes, it removed
many persons of a more thriving and consistent growth
in learning, then it either left there, or planted in their
steads; it medled not at all with a view or reformation of
those fundamental constitutions, on whose happy or
weak designations; the interest and prosperity, the decay
and ruin of such litterary Republicks principally depends,
as we shall shortly finde opportunity to demonstrate.

But the wishes of the most knowing and best men are
set far above these slender performances; they professe   30
(and I do but now make their sighings Articulat) that
the body of learning lyes scattered in as many peeces as
ever

ever *Medea* cut her little Brother into, and that they
are as hard to finde and re-unite as his was. That there
is no publick encouragement given to these gallant industries that endeavour to gather them up, and as much
as may be, recompose them: That we seem insensible
of that great Genius which animates and conducts this
present Age, and therefore sleight the discovery of that
in particular persons, who being many times big with
Heroick designes, perish for want of assistance in the de-
livery; or in case they be delivered, are found to have   10
wasted themselves in the production of a weak or a-
bortive infant, which otherwise might have been
strong and goodly: whereas men if they would but set
themselves to awaite and receive every glimpse and
dawning of knowledge (or at least cherish those that
would doe so) would finde it easie to bring it into a just
and beautifull body, and make an happy inversion of
that common saying, That our Ancients were Gyants,
and we are Dwarfs. And whereas some of the Heathen
wise men could say, That those were the best personages   20
that liv'd nearer, and lesse remoter from the Age of the
gods: we might contrarily by experience finde, that
we had made up the decayes of Humanity, and inforced
backe time into its first happy and lusty circle.

For if we looke into the life of man, take him in the
bare naked condition, in which Nature thrust him upon
earth, what a miserable helplesse thing shall we finde
him? miserabler in this then the bruits themselves, who
having at the most (though this also be denied with as
good reason as granted them) the use of a dim and   30
darke reason, or rather sense, and that in a direct line,
cannot be judges of their condition, and therefore consequently

sequently want the greatest ingredient of misery, the
sense of it; man is betrayed by his reason,(which cannot
be smothered in him, but that there wil be some sparks
and embers still alive) to a discerning of his sufferings
and some rude and unpolished wishes of a better condition; which if he can ever get into, it is meerly by the
collision of his naturall faculties, which strike out some
small sparkes to kindle that fuell: so that he being in a
manner in the condition of a Beast, hath no other way
to exempt himselfe from that misery and slavery, but   10
that little knowledge which chance, or the darke Axiomes of his owne reason can helpe him with.

And if againe we consider men gathering into the
Primitive societies, and assisting each other with
their mutuall endeavours and observations, we shall
finde that they come nearer civill Societies, by how
much they have made greater inroads into experience,
and were better versed in the acts of life. Nay, how
willing have they been to congratulate, yea Idolatrize
some of them, and put them into the lists of their   20
gods, (as wee may see out of the ruines of some
Histories which time hath not yet eaten up) for some
little inventions, which are at this day so common
with us, that they seem to be among the postulated
principles of nature, and to be borne with us; so that
these men who were ignorant of knowledge, and possibly would have sleighted it, if it had been offered to
them in its owne lustre; yet did live, subsist, and were
civilized by it.

But if we make a step further, and looke upon Com-   30
monwealths, how easie will it be to observe, that as
they flourished under the verdure, so have they withe-
                                                    red

red under the decay of Learning. Nor have they been
so fortunate under any governours as those who comming from a noble education, and a right observation
and deduction of things (which may well make a man
learned, though he never had seen a book) were neither
subject to these wilde evagations, nor savage rudenesses
which untutored Natures, through the want of a better
discipline, were apt to fall into.

Nay, if we looke somewhat more narrowly into
them, we may see that many private men born amidst   10
the dregs of the people, & not capable of any such high
hopes, have by this means far overtopped men of antiquity and ancient discent, and outvyed them with une-
quall services; whether by way of prevention, as old *Ap-
pius* a man wholly unacquainted with any systematicall
knowledge, in disswading the Romans from an inconsi-
derate peace they were about to shuffle up with *Pyrrhus*; or conservation, as that excellent reigne of *Au-
gustus*, one, who though his Cradle was not private,
yet in his first accesse to businesse, was not onely left in   20
a private capacity, but surrounded by an inimicall
faction: or if we look on augmentation what an illustrious time had *Rome* under *Trajan*, though a Spaniard,
that shee seemed to renew her age, and spread the
wings of her Eagle, where they could never have hoped to reach in her first period of greatnesse, which ever
after his dayes fell into a sensible and graduall weaknesse: not to note *Epaminondas* that god-like *Theban*,
who owed all his orient vertues to the light of the
Schooles, with whom (though he came from a vulgar   30
wombe) the greatnesse of his Country (as *Plutarch* observes) did shoot up and fade.

But

But if we would goe no further than the ornaments
and outward splendour of a place, what was it distin-
guished all the Pallaces in *Rome* and *Neroes* golden house
from the *Sabin* cottages, or the dwelling of *Publicola* ?
or the Imagery of *Greece* and Statues of *Corinth*, from
the first rude shapes of unpollished oake, but curiosity
and art; which yet notwithstanding had been vainly
hoped, if there had not been a concurrent humour of
men to entertaine and foster it; and this humour hath
been so fortunate to them, that notwithstanding time   10
hath defaced all the bounds of the *Roman* conquests,
and left them as invisible and inobservable, as the flight
of any bird that flew yesterday, yet in a few stones and
Medalls (not to mention the monuments of her intellectuall greatnesse) she hath left us such prints and mea-
sures, that we may justly trace and compute her (as he
did the Giants bulke by his thumbe) in her vast and stu-
pendous symmetry: whilst other Countries more remote from this greatnesse & happinesse that have not so
much as their ruines left them to vindicate them from   20
fables, and to testifie that they once were, live notwithstanding in all learned mouths, & that from the interest perhaps of one Citizen, whose merits hath made
him a part of posterity, and enabled him to a noble
gratitude to his Country, in rescuing her from the do-
tage and Tyranny of Time. And indeed without letters, and consequently the preservation and encouragement of them, to what a darknesse and mist should we
be confined, and in what a shadow should we live, a
darknesse worse then that of *Plato* his cave, when our   30
children, or childrens children, should be to seek for
what we know to day, & no observation be left to mankinde

kinde (for traditions must needs be in a few hands and
soone corrupt) to shorten the long journey of knowledge, and to bring it nearer an end: As we may see by
one example: The best man upon earth, and the onely more than man, spake and did so many things as all
the Volumnes in the world could scarce containe (as
one of his own Penmen witnesses of him) and yet there
is no more memory of them preserved amongst us, then
what is left in a very few sheets, not at all to mention
that Question, whether all the integrall parts of that   10
divine Book were preserved or no. Certaine we are
what a great losse we have in humane stories, and what
a large measure of Time, was either not described by
them, or not now to be found, so that in a *Trichotomy*
of Time made by the learnedst *Roman* sixteen hundred
years since, there was one part unknowne, and the
other fabulous; and yet sure we cannot but beleeve,
but that before mankinde had gleaned up some
litterature, and was softened and polished by it,
there were abundance of examples of either forti-   20
tude, and many invincible *Heroes* before *Achilles*, whose
Trophees are buried with them, and Triumphs forgot
as if they had never been seen, whilst those others that
remaine, must be accounted just such with us as the favour or envy of Poets and Historians are pleased to
make and represent them, so vast is the Preroga-
tive of letters, that they can dispense not onely life, but
estimation and glory unto whom they please, and command the reputation of past, and the beleefe of present
and future ages.   30

But to advance knowledge to its highest and truest
end, how necessary and subservient will it be to that
great

great designe of Religion, which without an immediate concourse and favour of Providence, can scarce either subsist without it, or preserve it selfe untainted
with gross errours, or distempered imaginations; how
serviceable may it be to many sublime mindes and refined understandings, that calling all things to an exact
Test of reason, wil not be brought to the acknowledge-
ment of their Maker, or the Truth of what is left con-
cerning him; if they be not guided by forcible demonstrations and porismaticall inferences of nature, which   10
may not precariously, but irresistibly infer a Deity;
and strong and naturall inductions of Reason: without
which, such mindes are but in vaine attempted, and
difficultly overcome: Or to goe further; how shall we
ever be sensible of the excellency and power of that
divine Book, which Gods owne finger hath wrote
and left us; if wee want ability and eyes to looke
upon the fulnesse and order of those Treasures;
Man indeed who is a determinate narrow thing,
must necessarily confine his thoughts to one subject,   20
and when he thinkes of one thing, of necessity desists
thinking of another. But God who is such a free infinity, can with one intuitive knowledge see all things,
and is the centre in every part of his circle. And therefore what he writes must needs be as universall as his
owne Spirit, and at one time communicate many
knowledges; whereas man can onely write of this or
that, and therefore it is unprofitable industry, not to
be undertaken without due assistances to attempt the
search of that Book, which like himself, hath an infinity   30
and immensity of knowledge in it. Not to speake of
the forme of it, which being writ in Tongues much
re-

removed from this place and age, and that surely with
all height of Elegance and fulnesse of expression; tis not
to be hoped for that any Translations can come up to it,
but that there must be abundance of exquisite knowledge smothered up in the Originall. Which though it
hath been studied and pursued, by numerous exalted
wits, & unwearied undertakers; yet we know that there
are abundance of ripe notions left to be found out by
future and latter endeavours, which shall never think to
want a Crown from this attempt, till this earth burn in   10
her funerall Pile, and we shall see all knowledge not in a
mist, but in a myrrour, and view the centre, the spring,
the root, the life of it *face to face*. Nor can I see what can
more heighten or beautifie this best Science, then the
regaining those Trophees from the Heathens which
they stole from us, who, though they knew not how
to use, yet triumphed in them: For all their glimmering
notions, were but lighted at our candle, although they
obscured and disguised them with false lights; yet by
that light did they shine to themselves and after ages,   20
who cannot but looke up with reverence at their ad-
vanced Natures, and wish they had been heightened by
a more noble principle, which had crowned all their
various Sciences with the principall Science, and in their
brave strayings after Truth, helpt them to better fortune than onely to meet with her handmaids, and kept
them from the fate of *Ulisses*, who wandring through
Hel, met all the ghosts, yet could not see the Queen. But
there is a strange Magneticall attraction in knowledge,
which plucks and draws the soule towards it, which is   30
just so much nearer its due repose, by how much it falls
nearer to this centre; And indeed it were a pity, that the
great

great Princesse of it should be lesse adorned, then some
of her subjects; and that *she who is all glorious within,*
should want *her garments of wrought gold and needlework,*
and not as well make her selfe glorious in the spoyles
of her enemies, as the *Israelites* steal away jewells from
the *Egyptians,* or *Solomon* fetch gold from *Ophir* to
adorn the Temple.

   I wish it were in my power, and your patience (most
Noble Senators) rather to view this intention, in its
many large particularities, then to propose it thus dead   10
coloured in a generall draught, which can like a *Mer-
cury* on the way, onely point but goe no further; But
truly tis enough for me a person, (hid in obscurity and
neglected into retirement) to make good wishes and
breath after these huge attempts, which I hope the
sublime disposer of all humane affaires, will as well put
into your hearts, as he hath put into your hands to ac-
complish. You have done great things for us, and
equall to what hath been done in any Nation, either
stoutly or fortunately. And if you will but now make   20
good our hopes in this one thing, you will put an end to
all our wishes, and settle us in a condition which will
somewhat resemble that eternall fruition which we all
breath after, a time of prayses.

   And indeed, if you were men that onely looked upon your selves, and studied no further then the propagation of your owne fame and interest. What better
means have you to confute all the scandalls and impu-
tations of your deadly adversaries, who have not spa-
red to speake you worse then *Goths and Vandalls,* and   30
the utter destroyers of all Civility and Literature, then
by seriously composing your selves to the designe of
                                                cherishing

cherishing of either. What directer caus-way could you finde to the aggrandization of your owne glory, then entertaining the celebrated care of so many Kings, the onely splendour of so many Republicks, the life and lustre of so many Ages? That which is certaine to make all brave men for the future, your admirers and followers, and to distinguish your Government from theirs, who being hurried by Confusion and Barbarisme, shall hereafter vanish into eternall forgetfulnesse. What better way to your profit, then to command abundance of fruitfull wits, which shall every day bud forth with some invention, serviceable either to the necessities of the poore, or graver magnificence of the rich? when mechanicall knowledge shall be multiplied and abbreviated, and you be able not onely to requite forreigne parts for the curiosities they have lent you; but also invite them hither to be your schollers, when there shall be a confluence of the finest industries among you, and he shall be accounted to want of due civill Accomplishments, that hath not come to perfect them from this place.

How serviceable will it be to you when you overflow with retired sagacities and raised industries, whom you may either for Gowne or Sword by land or sea employ upon all occasions; when you shall not need to put people in the places of greatest trust by reason of their Titular borrowed Gayety, but make use of such persons, as shall discover the greatest luxury and efflorescency of Vertue; Such persons who may succeed you in the seats where you now sit, (and may it be a fortunate Omen) exceed and outstrip your glories, such persons, which shall preserve us in a blessed peace;
wherein

wherein yet there shall be neither sloath nor luxury,
and either enlarge our Territories with wide forraigne
acquests, or else pull downe those powers which are
now the hate and burdens of the face of the earth.

But you that are men of sublime mindes, that have
carried you beyond all the doubts and objections of
flesh and blood, above the extent of your owne designes,
or almost the latitude of your owne wishes, beyond the
dictates of common Law and reason, will not give over
while there remains so great a worke. That God 10
who is abstract wisdome, and delights that his rationall
creatures should search after it, and that his Ministers
should study to propagate it, will expect that you
should be Foster-fathers of knowledge. He may punish
your naturall children with stupidity or ignorance, if
you doe not take the day while it is yours, to lead them
into the paths and Mazes of Science. And will he, think
you, forgive you (you being Fathers of the Publicke-
weale) if you forget those that are your children in
that relation? He cannot surely; he that is just will 20
expect from you the discharge of your duties,
which how it can be without a compleat taking care
of your charge your best selves can best consider.
But certainly it is none of the probablest wayes to
bring a people into a little shape of liberty, and free
their estates, from some small inconsiderable burdens,
and leave the better part of them, their mindes, no
more enlightned, no more tutoured, no more bur-
nished, than you at first found them. By this time
some may object, to what end I presse all 30
this. Have not wee Universities as famous as any
under Heaven? Is there not provision in this case
                                        enough?

enough? Have not our Ancestours been liberall beyond any of Europe ? will we violate their wills ? dis-
compose the present frame, before we be ascertained
what other to set up? beside running the Commonwealth into an unnecessary charge, and that for an unnecessary end, and in a time unfit, if not contrariant
to these designes, and that for an *Idæa* ?

Beleeve me these are pretty Objections, and till they
be confuted, very probable; but I beleeve well looked
into, they will according to the usuall ingenuity of 10
Truth, prove both to conduce to, and further this intention, and also to demonstrate unto you, that the thing
it selfe is so easie and feasible, that your selves cannot
without imputation of a grosse neglect, and ugly dis-
care of the Publick, avoid this consideration.

Tis true that our Universities for outward Magnificence, and a large, if not luxurious liberality, are equal,
if not superiour to any of those that we yet know of in
the lettered part of the world. They are venerable for
their antiquity, and have a long time thriven under the 20
indulgency of the past ages, & been ennobled by the production of many rare and divine personages, who have
made more illustrious the whole Nation. But whether
in generall their Statutes be so exact and refined, as
may satisfie the need and curiosity of this exalted age,
or that our Accademies at the present teach either all,
or the gallantest Theories of knowledge, will be seene
anon. And that being once made evident, it will not
be hard to inferre, that other Universities of a later
standing and poorer subsistance, have both in extent of 30
knowledge, and multiplicity of excellent persons, been
able to equall, if not out-doe them. Nay that those
pre-

present Revenues whereupon they now surfeit, have choaked abundance of active Industries, nay beene a meanes to thrust into Ecclesiastical or Litterary offices a many of persons, who had they been suffered to obey their owne inclinations, and followed some Trade or Handicraft, might have ranked themselves amongst the ablest of their Profession; Whilst others who had soules more towardly and capable, were by such Drones as these kept out of the Hives, and either for- 10 ced to seek their food from afar, or else sit downe (un- lesse provided for by their Parents) with no other gaine by their Philosophy and Reason, then a few Stoicall sentences in the contempt of wealth, and the commendations of poverty.

Now that there is provision enough, we shall both grant, and by it take occasion to insinuate, that the State need not multiply any of her expences in pur- suance of this wish. All our suit is, that these endow- ments, and pious liberality, may be converted into uses suitable to the ends of the Donors, and tend rather 20 to a publicke advantage, then to the private fostering of a many idle Pedantick Brotherhoods. It now lies like mucke, and possibly is noysome to the place where it is, but spread it abroad, it will manure all the Land, and returne the increase of an unvaluable and happy har- vest. There is none requires it to another use, but one- ly to a better use, and in the end it can be no more rob- bery, then tis sacriledge to rescue a Temple from the superstition wherewith it was defiled, to the use of a purer and more illuminated Religion. 30

I must needs confesse, (and I speake it with a deale of Religion to the memory of them that are gone before

us,

us,) that among the many good examples they have left
to this Nation, their liberality, if not profusenesse, in
things of this nature hath not been the least. But then
I beseech you, Honourable Worthies, consider in
what times they lived; they were darke, beset
with mists of ignorance and superstition, and they
could onely direct their charity that way so far as they
knew it best. Their Ordinances and cautions, were, no
doubt in their times, full of excellent wisdome and
deep reason. But since they ceased to be mortall, it hath   10
pleased the Son of Righteousnesse to breake through
the clouds which shadowed their ages, and to let us
have more of day. And as the Sun here below doth
not onely in his rescuing the light, discover himselfe,
but also guilds and discloses all about him; so that eternall Sun, when he opens himselfe, opens at the same
time all humane and inferiour knowledge, which is
still more or lesse visible, as his rayes shine on it, or
withdraw from it. Now he having every day made
greater appearances of himselfe; humane learning   20
hath also been more enlightned; and he is not acquainted with the Businesse of knowledge, that knows not
what sensible increases (I had almost said perfections)
it hath of late arrived to. So that what means was
used before to preserve it from perishing, and to propagate it, must how be used for augmentation, and
splendor. What means were used to keep it in a few
hands in a corner (like a great exile, thrust away by a
contrary power) till some better times, must now be
used to disperse it through the face of the earth, and to   30
make it tread as far as mankinde. What meanes were
used before, for a bare historicall knowledge, must
                                                        now

now be turned into a censorious justice upon ov'r old
opinions, and into severe an eager disquisitions of new
truths; for knowledge hath no limits nor Land-marks
but being ubiquitary, and therefore desirous to diffuse it
selfe, she endeavours by all means her promotion and di-
latation. Nor doth she ever meet with any that would
enlarge her Empire, but shee ambitiously encourages
them, and willingly crownes them. Now for any one
to thinke, that one and the same meanes are to be used
to preserve a State, either new curdled and moulded   10
into forme, or else by outward violence retired to its
last seat and almost first principles, and the same state
when it hath overcome either its infancy or misery,
and like a wakened Gyant begins to rowze it selfe up,
and looke where it may conquer, is utterly unvers'd in
the affaires of the world, and below instruction.

And doubtlesse, upon these considerations, were it
possible that these happy soules could either returne
hither, or were it suitable to their blessednesse to
minde things that are done under the Moone, they   20
could not but joyne with any that would undertake to
serve them in so pious an ingagement, as to make their
contributions more excellently serviceable to the ends
they purposed. And therefore we cannot thinke it any
more violation to their will, at all to advance their
provisions to their owne ends by better wayes, then
we thinke that you (Noble Senators) are parracides to
your Country in rescinding those Lawes which your
Predecessors made, yet through length of time, and
rapine of those in whose care they lay, began contrary   30
to their first intention, rather to oppresse, then defend
and releeve us. For so long as humane reason is weake

and

and imperfect, it can never provide any Lawes against all circumstances of chance, length of time, fraud and weaknesse of mankinde, but it will bring forth a *necessity* to repeale them, equall, if not superiour to that which first enacted them.

For discomposition of the present frame, may not, I pray this be a Topicke for any Government, though never so ill grounded, never so irregular, or never so Tyrannicall? Should we sit still, and expect that those in whose hands it is, should quietly resigne it, or new-mould it themselves, or some fine chance should do it to our hands? or should we not out of this very reason, if our houses were all untiled and obvious to all injuries of the weather, forbeare to pull them down or mend them, because we would make no alteration, and so continue in our miserable patience, because we feare a change and some trouble; like *Æsops* Plowman crying to *Jupiter*, to helpe our cart out of the mire, and we never put to a hand? or should we expect that some Deity, or unthought of influence would rescue us from these inconveniences which we saw, but would not remove? I am afraid whether any can be serious upon this question: For as happinesse is the reward of courage and industry; so what ever people ever yet obtained any Reformation without sweat or wounds, and a just violence to the over-ruling power; just I say, though it clashed with the letter of some *Positive* Law for with the *Fundamentall* and true ends of government it could not. But there is no need in this case to urge this so hard to you, who so nobly brake through this objection, and redeemed the supreme power, which being now so indisputable in your hands:

This

This wish requires no more of you then the exercising
of it, wherein you will onely finde opposition from
those who have endeavoured to blast, and yet continue
a will to defeat and maligne your best actions. Nay, and
(I hope you will give me leave to mention it for your
Honours) we are encouraged rather to presse this
from your owne example of magnanimity, and zeale
in whipping those high Priests, and buyers and sellers
out of our Temple, and that when your power was
in umbrage, that now you will (when it hath obtai- 10
ned its just light and fulnesse) employ it on so easie a
taske, as this last peece of Reformation; which will
embalme your memories, and leave almost nothing to
your Successours to doe piously or justly. That this
turne of time may not be capable of such a noble alteration, I am not afraid from the best comparison
and recollection of times and reasons, not onely to
deny, but even to evince the contrary. For what
more seasonable opportunity can we have, then that
we see the highest spirits, pregnant with great mat- 20
ters, and in despite of these Tumults and Troubles
which inviron them of every side, labouring with
somewhat, the greatnesse of which they themselves
cannot tell, and with a wonderfull deale of courage,
attempting the discovery of a new world of knowledge? These bodings cannot be of nothing, but upon
a narrower recognition will appeare full of miracle,
which amounts with me to no lesse then the chasing
away of shadows before the breake of the great day.
God surely, that begins a fuller manifestation of him- 30
selfe, suffers us to approach him by these degrees, and
therefore hath diffused a great and a restlesse Genius

in

in this age, far greater then any hath been of a long
time. And as Astrologers say, that there are at some
certaine times some powerfull influences showred by
the conjunction or positure of some Planets, which if
they be not received and magically applied at that
very time, do immediately passe away, and become
ineffectuall, and are not to be expected againe, till after many ages; so any tract of time, when it meets a
sublime and elevated spirit to assist and guide it, cannot certainly without disadvantage and losse, refuse   10
to entertaine it; nay they cannot be so stupid, as not
to thinke both that the time is unregainable, and that
a judgement awaits them for being so bold as to resist
the discoveries of it. But I cannot thinke so ill of
these men among whom I was borne, that they will
shut their eyes against this light that breaks so
brightly and glistringly in upon them, and be lethar-
gically content to please themselves with the reverend
follies and dreams of their forefathers.

Tis no matter what some frozen Sadduces, or some
others of a worse name if there be any, can scoffe,   20
that it is folly to entertaine any such vaine imaginations, and madnesse to prosecute them: Tis folly will
prove the happiest wisdome, and no more a deviation
of the understanding, then the entertaining a new naturall exact scheame of heaven, and nature, in lieu of
the old broken interfering *Hypotheses*, which rely on
no other probability but asent of sense, distorted by
education, and brawned by custome.

Tis no matter, what some purblinde Polititians, or   30
sneaking worldlings talke of the difficulty of times,
and say, that these soft aires of peace, cannot be heard
                                                amidst

amidst the loud musicke of Warre, and that mens
thoughts, are too much broken and harrassed to fall
upon these things, which must be the fruits of the
deepest and most silent leasure, You have the highest
destiny favouring your designes, put an end to all
such Tumults; and we have now no more of War then
is necessary to the preservation of our peace, which
seems to smile on us againe, and promise us, that she
will not flye away, for fear lest her snowy garments
should be stayned in blood.   10

But put the case that your Enemy were as visible
and powerfull as ever, yet I dare be knowne to thinke,
that it were much more honourable for you to assume
these thoughts: nay that they both were not
inconsistent together. What can you imagine to doe
more worthy of memory, or imitation, then in the
midst of your most urgent dangers to lay a modell, and
draw the lines of happinesse and security for all posterity? How can you better demonstrate your selves
fearlesse and hearty, in what you goe about, then by   20
shewing such a severity and composition of spirit; nay
such a contrary neglect of what opposition is set before you, as to minde those vast designes of litterall
magnificence, or further acquisition? What more
shining in all the Annalls of *Rome*, then the porten-
tuous bravery of sending Forces into *Spaine*, when
Hanniball was at the Gates, and selling that field
whereon he encamped at so deare a rate, as it would
have passed at, had he been prisoner within the walls,
and his Army dispersed? yea (and to shew that these   30
later times want not parallels of the Ancient Gran-
deurs) what will be more illustrious in the History of
                                                    Holland,

Holland, then their high and visible cares, and almost prodigall magnificence for learning, while as they yet strugled with a sad war, and had not yet released their necks, from the sway of a perfidious and horrid Tyrant ?

For the people whom you are to care for, it cannot be but that peace might have softened and emasculated them, whereas their calamities have brought them into a better agility and constitution, to promote their excellent desires to liberty in any thing which they may conceive really conducible; and there is no cause to doubt, but they will facilly be swayed by that power under whose valorous conduct they have asserted themselves from all impressions and marks of dishonour and slavery, which usurpation, iniquity of time, or forreigne force had put upon them.

It cannot be denied, but by the invaluable losse of bloud and Treasure, the body of this Nation is become thin and leane, and therefore he were a Viper that would offer to gnaw or suck it any more (for any farther pressure, be it never so little is now excessive) and therefore it would be but just to wave a Petition for any publicke contribution (though possibly there hath been some liberality exercised to worse ends, which had it been directed this way, might have equalled any of the ancient magnificencies and honourable profusenesses upon learning) although if you were urged to some small liberality, or rather prevented any suit for it, it would be a huge furtherance to what is desired of you, yet we onely beg; nay conjure you by all that is deare to you, or desired of you, that you will imploy this which you finde already

ready left to your hands, and doe these things without any charge, and onely lend us your Authority, to
doe this longed for worke; and no doubt if you cannot, or will not lend any fewell to it, God will stir
up the hearts of many private persons, and inflame
them with equall intentions, and make their hands
bring it in in a full measure.

And now that which remaines of me to doe (for I
conceive I have quitted my selfe of the Objections,
and therefore may dismisse them) will be a triple   10
taske. First, to shew how farre the state of our Universities needs a reformation. Secondly, how it may
be brought about: And thirdly, I shall particularize
some ends which I have transiently before glanced at,
not as ends, but as fruits and enjoyments of your
noble piety. And herein I shall the rather be short,
because these being at the most, but the best sort of
wishes, I shall observe that course which the best
men do in their devotions, to pray for the best things
they can, yet not limit the power they pray to, to   20
such or such a way of granting their requests, as being
resolved by what meanes soever it comes, to receive it
chearfully, and knowing that power which they ad-
dresse themselves unto, cannot onely doe it in a better manner then they can thinke of, but in a fuller.

For the first: I could never yet make so bad an *Idæa*
of a true University, as that it should serve for no
nobler end, then to nurture a few raw striplings, come
out of some miserable Country-school, with a few
shreds of Latine, that is as immusicall to a polite ear as 30
the gruntling of a Sow, or the noise of a Saw can be
to one that is acquainted with the Laws of harmony.
And

And then possibly before they have survayed the
Greeke Alphabet, to be racked and tortured with a
sort of harsh abstracted logicall notions, which their
wits are no more able to endure, then their bodies the
Strapado, and to be delivered over to a jejune barren
Peripatetick Philosophy, suited onely (as *Mounsieur
Des-Cartes* sayes) to wits that are seated below Medi-
ocrity, which will furnish them with those rare imaginations of *Materia prima, Privation, Universalia,* and
such Trumpery, which they understand no more then   10
their Tutors, and can no more make use of in the affaires of life, then if 3000. yeares since they had run
through all the Hierogliphicall learning of the
Egyptians, and had since that time slept in their *Mum-
my,* and were now awaken. And then as soone as
they have done licking of this file, to be turned to
graze in poor *Ethicks,* which perhaps tell them as
much in harder words, as they had heard their Mo-
thers talke by the fire-side at home. Then are they
turned loose, and with their paper-barks committed   20
to the great Ocean of Learning; where if they be
not torne, they returne backe so full of desperation
and contempt of their profession, and sad remem-
brance of their youth so trivially spent, that they hate
all towardly engagements that way, and suffer themselves either to sinke in a quagmire of idlenesse, or to
be snatched away in a whirlepool of vice. But in case
some with much adoe get a shore (for a long or a far
voyage upon these termes they cannot make) and by
the foresaid means stilt themselves into some professi-   30
on; what deplorable things (unlesse it be those few
which Nature makes for ostentation to be jewells in
this

this earth) prove they, in filling the world with de-
testable quacking Empericks, lewd, and contentious,
Gown-men, or ignorant mercenary Divines?

Againe, I have ever expected from an *University*,
that though all men cannot learne all things, yet they
should be able to teach all things to all men, and be
able either to attract knowing men from abroad out
of their owne wealth, or at least be able to make an
exchange. But how far short come we of this, though I
acknowledge some difference between our Universities? 10
We have hardly Professours for the three principall
faculties, and these but lazily read, and carelesly followed. Where have we any thing to do with Chimi-
stry, which hath snatcht the keyes of Nature from the
other sects of Philosophy, by her multiplied experiences? Where have we constant reading upon either
quick or dead *Anatomies*, or ocular demonstration of
herbes? Where any manuall demonstrations of Mathematicall Theorems or Instruments? Where a promotion of their experiences, which if right carried on, 20
would multiply even to astonishment? Where an exa-
mination of all the old *Tenets*? Review of the old experiments & traditions which gull so many *junior* beliefs,
and serve for nothing else but for idle Priests, to make
their Sermons more gaudy? Where is there a solemn
disquisition into History? A nice and severe calculation
and amendment of the *Epochs* of time? Where a survey
of Antiquities, and learned descants upon them? Where
a ready and generous teaching of the Tongues? Free
from Pedantisme, and the impertinencies that that kind 30
of learning hath been pestered with? And all this done
not by some stripling yongster, who perhaps under-
stands

stands that which he professes as little as any thing
else, and mounts up into the chaire twice or thrice a
yeare, to mutter over some few stolne impertinencies,
but by some stayed man, of tryed and known abilities
in his profession, allured by a competent encouragement to stay in the University, who may at certaine
times read, at certaine times attend the resolution of
doubts, offering directions at other times, and ingaging
them in sober and rationall disputes, in which being
restrained from sophistry, they may chase and polish   10
their endowments, and whet one the other by praise or
emulation.

If we finde very few, or perhaps none of them in
our Universities, I suppose I offer no violation nor in-
jury to their hoarinesse and venerable fame, if I say, they
are capable of farther promotion, and that they have
not yet arrived to the exactnesse of the Jesuits
Colledges, and many transmarine Universities, the
latter of which, if not the former, they far exceed in
pecuniary endowments and outward statelinesse.   20

And truly, but that I would not doe violence to the
Mother that bare me, and prophane that place which is
in my account holy, I could lay open abundance of
their customes, both superstitious, irrationall, uncivill,
and ridiculous; I could instance how some vices are
growne generall in some degrees of them, how many
slugs there are, how some courses they take will prove
meerly the choaking of all literature. But since this
would amount to a long rabble, and degenerate into
some *Satyre* or *Pasquill*, rather then an *Areopagitick*, I   30
will be content, having a publicke businesse in hand, to
lay aside all bitternesse, though it might be advantagious

gious to my purpose, and with due meeknesse and
equanimity, draw to my last taske, and then sit downe
with silent wishes and earnest expectation.

Two things then I have to beg; some assistances
that you would give the Universities from themselves,
and some assistance that you would give them from
without themselves. From themselves: that you would
reduce those Frier-like Lists of Fellowships into a fewer
number, and those that you retaine, to be bestowed on
men, excellent in their particular endowments, and   10
peculiar for some use or other, that so the number
of the Professours might encrease, and all of them
be enabled to prosecute the hints and *impetus* of their
owne inclinations, and others of more patient heads
be tyed to instruct those severall persons which should
make addresses to them; a third possibly, worne out
with contemplations and those greater labours of the
minde, might sit warme, and know nothing lesse then
Necessity in their honoured old age. Sixe Fellowships thus ordered, with a sufficient allowance and en-   20
couragement would be more advantagious, and contribute more to the raising up of the despised head of
Learning, then sixscore at this present doe; while the
remaining portion of Revenues might be sequestred by
a select Committee of able and knowing men (wherein
some Representatives of the University should be
mingled) to be changeable and accountable every
yeare: to be disposed of, for examining and pursuing
experiments, encouragements of honour, compleating
and actuating some new inventions, supplying the nee-   30
dy ones that really wanted these wings to take great
flights, relieving of strangers; and lastly, provoking
some

some sydereall and flaming soules to display themselves in their full and radiant meridian lustre. For then will it prosper with Learning, when rewards fit themselves to men, and men are not forced to distort themselves to rewards; when every mans *Genius* moves in its owne orbe, and is not hurried aside in an *eccentrick* motion.

From without the Universities: that you would thinke of some better way of disposing those few Colledges which are thinly scattered up and downe the land, and make them either collaterall or subservient to this designe; whereas now they are of little or no other use then to nourish the supine idlenesse of a few *Lurdans*, and foment their illitterate debates, tossed to and fro among them without any delight to any but those who love bawling and canvasing such unlearned opinions which runne in this circle without end, and contribute not the least to the promotion or discovery of Truth.

Secondly, that as you would (with all due provision for the civill peace) take off that hatefull *gagg* of licencing which silences so many Truths, and frights so many ingenuities, and makes them abhorre the publick; so you would put such a gentle imposition upon Books, that upon every Impression two might goe to the publicke Library; and that forreigne Bookes, brought over hither in any number, might doe the like, or at least at some reasonable rate.

Thirdly, that all the Medalls, Statutes, ancient Rings, and other Antiquities, pictures of learned delight, or famous men, that either were the late Kings or any other persons whose estates stand confiscate to you, might

might be appropriated this way. For by a cheaper and more generous magnificence you cannot endeare your selves to all the lovers and sons of knowledge, and carefull Patrons of mankinde; nor secure the memory of your noble acquests by more illustrious Trophees.

And lastly, since that this Island can no more possesse all the Treasures of knowledge then it can the Treasures of the earth, that you would be ready to cast all respect and honour upon learned forreigners, although you use no largesse towards them. Men that through a thirst of fame have beguiled themselves into large and divine contemplations, cannot but thinke they reap a great fruit of their labours, and be surprized with it, when they see themselves smiled upon, and courted by such a mighty State, and be ambitious to disperse their Theories there, where they see they are so much honoured. Now how by this policy your Brethren of *Holland*, have in a manner monoplized all the sparkling wits of Europe; there are many that sit among you that can best informe you. Nor is there yet any apparent reason to me why you should not also studde and embosse *this* Nation with them. Now to what more particular designe all this should levell. There have been so many modells, and those so various, though to the same end, chalked out by the greatest ingenuities, that it would be very hard (lov'd I transcriptions or largenesse never so well) to represent them all, each one abounding in his owne sense, and so possibly not so servient to the designations of another. It shall be enough for me (waving my judgement or disquisition of them) to set downe the resultance of a many diligent observations and iterated thoughts;

thoughts; which as they have not strayed too much into wilde *Idea's*, so I know not why they may not be
more particularly fitted for our elevation.

First, I have considered that an endeavour to bring
all persons under the sway of knowledge, could not
but approach very neare a *Platonicke* Commonwealth,
and must in the triall enervate the people, and call
them from those necessary professions of Tillage and
War, and make them acquainted with the artifices of
delight. Besides there were but a few inclinations so   10
noble, as could overlooke the grosse entertainments
of sense, and aime at a more pure and intellectuall
happinesse. And among these men I found particular
Temperatures as it were, and some secret *Sympathies*
and *Antipathies* to some, or some particular studies,
whilst there were very few intellectuall *complexions*
that desired all; and these enjoyed not the particulars
so fully as those that bent that particular way.   I
found also that many men rudely educated, and such
as would have proved no great Clerkes, though they   20
had been bred up in the Pedanticke way of the
Schooles, had notwithstanding through long and
fore observation, so well tutored their reason, that
they proved many times persons fitter for businesse
then those that had the assistance of much unprofitable literature. I had seen also some men after many
yeares spent in the world, begin to retire into themselves, and as seriously and effectually as they could
apply themselves to Books, which yet was commonly ineffectuall to them, if not quickned with some   30
live-voyce and knowing assistance.

From this masse of observations I fell to consider
                                              thus,

thus, That if Man were a creature both so excellent
and active, it were but justice to him that the naturall
vergency of his *Genius* should be found out and assisted;
and that surely could not be in any better time then
in his infancy at the dawning of his reason, when he
could not be employed any other way, and his inno-
cency made him most susceptible of any impression or
figure. And if at such a time, then surely he was to
be assayed by most easie trialls, and that by pleasant
pastimes of sense, and not by any harsh abstractions   10
or rough discipline. Yet those recreations of his I
thought ought to be such as should be profitable, and
able to furnish his maturer thoughts with some solid
Idæas and sound representations of things. And here
I made account I had found the right path, which our
Schooles having so long left, was the reason they
were so seldome prosperous or fruitfull in great matters. Well, this being so, those that had spent their
childhood thus, I supposed, might with much more
advantage and ease, retire into a more ignoble calling;   20
and those whom some harder fortune alienated to o-
ther employments, might carry such grounds away
with them, as might conduct and dispose their observations all their lives after; whilst all those who had
a greater vivacity of spirits, might be set apart to
worthy and suitable employments, and none be des-
paired by ill methods, or tyrannicall Tutors.

Thus far had I got, and there remained this with
me; That those men that were set apart for knowledge
must busie themselves about two things, either about   30
the dispersing, or augmentation of it: And about dispersing of it, there could be no better meanes then to
make

make it easie and amiable; and this brought me to beleeve that that education would thrive the best in any
place, that was the least cumbred with unnecessary
notions, and did the most facilly and orderly insinuate
it selfe into the understanding; and I tooke the duty
of a Master to endeavour these two. Besides, I considered that that was the best which was the most reall
and universall: and then I perceived that it was better
to grave *things* in the mindes of children, then *words*,
for I had knowne some great speakers, though in- 10
discreet, gazed on onely as strange sights and Parrats,
where as I could not imagine, but that if a wise man
came into any Country, whose language he had never
heard, he would by his deportment and insinuations
make a shift to be entertained and respected. And
this made me suppose, that many men that could
count their languages by this fingers, might possibly
be of no more use among mankinde, then so many
Apes or Magpies. But such whose mindes were
strengthened with realities, were onely men, and in- 20
deed so much men, as they were masters of the true
use of reason, and knew how to guide it; and that to
them, Languages must of necessity adde beauty and
perfection, and acquaint them with a much of knowledge which was never writ in their mother Tongue.
And since that there were some men who would
fortunately learn and teach the knowledge of others,
though they could not augment it much themselves;
I judge that nature did principally intend these for dis-
pensators and conveighers of it. And others of more 30
vast and capacious intellectualls, that could never be
bounded by the Theories of one other, were onely fit
for

for augmentation; and because there were some pro-
pensions and aversions, of which they themselves
could not well render an account, which if disobeyed
succeeded untowardly and unsuccessefully; I presently
inferred, that the *genius* of each one was to be employed and cherished in its owne kinde; and that there
was seldome any great matter to be expected from it,
if *preternaturally* diverted, or dispersed into many various thoughts and designes, which did onely distract
and weaken it.   10

But when once I began to take a prospect of the
whole Landscap of Knowledge, Methought there was
much of it moorish and fennish, much of it overgrown
with thornes and brambles, and some parts of it had
not been justly measured, nor indeed fully discovered,
so that I thought it would be too stupid humility, to
rest with the traditionall wisdome of our Ancestours,
and not to looke after further enlargement and advancement. For there being much of it uncultivated
and unmanured; I saw there was abundantly left,   20
for to provoke and satisfie each future industry, which
how they should be employed, I could not better tell
how to designe then thus; first, considering the excellency of Man, and the restlesse activity of his understanding, and the strange volutations of his affaires, I
thought the actions of so noble a creature deserved
far better, then to be covered in oblivion. And because experience was nothing but a sober deduction
and summing up of many observations, and man was
an apish imitative thing; I thought there was nothing 30
better to abreviate the length of observation, and to
furnish him with good copies which he should fol-
                                                    low,

low, then being acquainted with past actions and times,
and conversing with the images of the bravest persons
that went before. And truly, all this, I for a while
flatter'd my selfe, was supplyed us out of those Histories which as yet survive. But after some acquaintance with them, I began to quit this beliefe; for I
found many of them clash, many of them rent, many
ridiculous, most composed to pleasure, and therefore
not descending to those particularities and circumstances, without which a History is but dead, and a   10
bare *Skeleton* without either flesh or sinewes. Besides a
many of them seemed to flourish up into *Ideas*, and
others were so larded and pestred with the private
discourses and conceptions of their Writers, that
they seem to have been composed for no other end.
Besides most of them were but Summaries and Epitomes, so that those deductions which were drawne
from them, were not so pertinent, but fallible, and
such as seemed rather to follow the conceptions of
the Observatour, then to be naturally enforced from   20
the things themselves. For this cause I began to wish
that there were a place in some University appointed
for a collection of all such Papers, Letters, Tran-
scripts, and Relations, which should discover the in-
ner side of Negotiations, and events, and the true face
of things, without the adulteration of common policy. And I thought it were profitable rather to take
in many needlesse things, then to leave out one need-
full, because a judging minde out of many particularities, could draw a better estimate of things, and de-   30
duce more certaine, and unquestioned axiomes.

But because Man is a creature of such infinite variety,

riety, and that in every one, there is somewhat shining and excellent; I wished that some laudable diligence, had gathered a catalogue of Characters, and that
of the lives of some of the more eminent; which I
should not care, how much they had been stuffed
with particular actions, because Man in businesse is
but a Theatricall person, and in a manner but perso-
nates himselfe, but in his retired and hid actions, he
pulls off his disguise, and acts openly. So that I judged
by that meanes that Characters were the best and 10
faithfullest to be gained, and we should come to a
righter knowledge and judgement of Vertue, and the
Passions. For I had seen abundance of things related
as high acts of generosity, which possibly were but
the effects of weaknesse, cruelty and despaire. And
withall seeing onely the greatnesses of some men
mentioned, and neither their particular imperfections, nor the meanes by which they atchieved their
ends particularly set downe; I thought it could not
but stretch many weake mindes to disproportionate 20
thoughts; and like *Palmerine* or *Don Quixote* make
them thinke of things beyond the Moon. Therefore
did I conceive it necessary to trace these Grandees as
much as may be, through all their windings and hid-
den paths.

But because men must walke upon the earth, and
needs receive those influences which are shed from
heaven, and therefore exceedingly differ according to
their severall climes; I thought not onely an exact
description of the severall Countries was to be ob- 30
tained, and if it were possible, all their secret myste-
ries, and retired criticismes of state; that so, obser-
vative

vative mindes, might have farre richer stuffe, and variety of formes whereupon to work. And also there
might probably by this meanes in length of time, be
found out severall satisfactory reasons, and wayes of
discovering and judging the many inclinations and natures of men: And so by that means a greater facilitation of businesse, and possibly greater successe in it,
then have yet commonly happened.

Moreover, Man that had solely the use of reason,
and by it was separated from other creatures, I
thought had all the interest in the world to endeavour the perfection of it, and the severall wayes of its
best advantages. And this I thought, was no better
way attempted, then if the veynes of things were
rightly and naturally cut up, and he had such principles placed within him, as would without any di-
sturbance or confusion assist him in the pursuance of
any Truth, or in the examining of any thing doubt-
full. This I thought had been done by *Logick* (as they
call it) but there the *Predicaments* were so untowardly ranged, that a mans minde shall not without some
hesitation know where to fasten; and then when he
hath pitched there, he is but engaged in a dispute.
But I beleeve had the dissection beene naturall, the
minde would instantly have pitched right, and then
have been inabled to have weilded that Notion to
her best use. Here I expected reliefe from *Metaphy-
sicks*, but they were so abstrusely abstract, and so far
remote from use, that they seemed to hurry the
minde too far away, and make it too volatile and
aery, and so difficultly attainable, that halfe a life
need to be severely spent in learning them. But the
con-

conduct of reason which I wished for, I wished naturall and easie, and such as might gently sinke into
younger mindes, and be there imbraced with no im-
pulsion; but the delight which commonly tickles the
soule when she meets with any radiant and pregnant
Truth. This made me imagine highly of the *Mathematicks* for the clearnesse of their grounds and excellent building upon them; but these were withdrawne
from Quantity, and besides had the liberty to make
their owne suppositions, which to morall and politick   10
reason (which was to judge of things as it found them
distracted into many casualties and circumstances) was
denied; and therefore that there was but little advantage to be had this way, so that I could not de-
vise any better meanes then to make the minde pliant
and passible to any Truth, to free her from all these
inquinated prejudices of education, tradition, or
childish observation, and then withall to plant such a
doubtfulnesse in her, as should not easily ascent to any
one thing which was not fortified with strong reason   20
and right experience. And to doe this, there cannot
but be extream necessity of a person not meanly vers'd
in the causes of errour, and stratagems of reason, who
should dig out such *axioms* as should rectifie the mind,
and lead her by the hand, in the most subtile contemplations, and so refine her, that she might be able to
extract pure and large *Theories* out of things most im-
mers'd and hid in matter.

For the *Mathematicks* themselves, I found them full
of excellent variety and harmony, strongly fenced   30
with their owne Truth, and branched out into many
admirable inferences and productions. But yet methought

thought that there was somewhat in them which
was yet hid from us, and that the ancient foun-
ders of these sciences had been content to retaine
somewhat not fully discovered. For I found most
men imployed onely in learning those immense heaps
of Demonstrations *they* had left us, but seldome enlarging them or going forward, which made me fear that
the key of these Sciences were hid, and that without
such a key, or engine it had been unpossible to reare up
such a huge super-structure of vast consequences. But   10
this I found two or three great spirits had already light
on, and had directed a way which if well followed,
will make our *Mathematicall* reason nimble and apt to
finde the fountain head of every *Theoreme*, and by degrees, as we may hope, inable us to the solution of any
Probleme without any more assistance then pen and
inke (so that a man may carry all these admirable
Sciences about him) and direct us to more exact and
easie instruments then any have been yet knowne, and
recall mens minds by delicate ravishing contemplati-   20
ons, from the sordid jugling use of those instruments on
which they now so perversly and unanimously doat.

But when I once begun seriously to view that
strange disposition of things which we call Nature;
I could not even in my ruder estimation of it but be
much astonished. For it was plaine to me there was
more art and prodigious workmanship in a Gnat or
a Fly then there was in the greatest engines or productions of man; which if they were not casually
found out, were but the meere promotions and pursu-   30
ances of Nature. By this I took my self deeply engaged
for to looke upon that Fabricke with more curiosity
and

and diligence then they commonly use, who judge
and suppute every thing according to the outward
tickling and blandishments of sense. And as to this
designe, I thought I was well provided for, by those
many volumnes of naturall Philosophy, which I found
to flatter me with a many large and braving Titles. And
I thought that when I was once well acquainted with
them, I should have had my minde fitted for excellent
notions, and embellished with such rich principles, as
could not but furnish me with a many excellent and   10
sweet deductions. But when I had spent some time thus,
and began to shake off that implicite faith which must
for a while binde up learners, and discovered what con-
tradictions, loose conceptions, and endlesse controver-
sies those Volumnes were fraught with, I perceived I
had gained nothing else but a multitude of vaine spe-
culations, which in all reason of the world I ought to
dis-beleeve. About this time I happened to bee acquainted with a sort of books that denounced a sharpe
warre against the old Philosophy, and very severely   20
undertooke to put it all under the sponge, and withall
to raise up such other new observations as should
prove more handsomely, and truely make up the ap-
parences and changes of Nature. These men I hugged,
and indeed expected from them, some performances
equall to my expectations; but then againe I found
that man may be farre more happy in discovering of
errours then in finding out of Truths. For some of
those Treatises were meerly draughts and designations,
others violently wrested the explaining of things to   30
their owne principles, and rather forced Nature to
their conceptions, then enlarged their conceptions as
wide

wide as Nature. Othersome there were, who abusing a
Philosophicall liberty, strayed into some anticke
Theories, and made Nature monstrous: Others laid
down very probable and neat *Hypotheses*, but absolutely
unsuited to the nature of the thing; so that I collected,
that though we had made some steps forwards, yet we
were not at our journies end. And because I saw that
a many curious notions were but like spiders webs, and
that experiences have the greatest light, I thought we
were principally to insist upon that way. But because 10
most experiments were found out rather casually then
by Philosophicall reasoning, and some men out of one
small observation could be bold to raise abundance of
vaine consequences, and for one and the same experi-
ment, there were sundry reasons brought, and it was
easily wrested, and salved by divers principles, I judged
that as there was an extreame deale of diligence and
nicity to the practicall pursuance of Nature, so, that it
was not safe to draw any one principle from any one
observation, unlesse there could not possibly be any o- 20
ther reason given for it, or else alike discoveries had
confirmed it, that if any other interpretation were put
upon it, it was unproper and vaine: For as it is easie for
men of acute wits to mis-judge and mis-expect Nature;
so when an *axiom* is rightly gained, it is easie to work
it up, and to draw from it many strange and magicall
Productions.

And because there are abundance of extraordinary
appearances both at home and abroad, I judged it necessary, that all these should be carefully gathered and 30
registred; so that those many varieties comming into a
long Catalogue, and digested by a sober minde, might
afford

afford many rare and beautifull discoveries of the glory of their Creator.

What other meanes might be used both in this and *Medicine*, would be too large now to insist on, since I at first purposed but a *Synopsis*, which, I cannot despair my selfe, if it were rightly or hotly pursued, could not but bring forth a more plentifull harvest then we at the present expect. There are, no doubt, many of nobler thoughts, who might furnish you with more exact and high designations; and truly, I shall thinke 10 my selfe abundantly satisfied, if, from these poore reflections, you may be invited to take their advice, and follow their vast and judicious considerations in this nature. However for my part let this *humble Essay* be as much neglected or revil'd as may be, I shall sit down quiet with a conscience of the discharge of my duty, though it can reap no farther, then the putting of these wishes upon the file, and transmitting them to Posterity.

These things, as I have but briefly touched, so to par- 20 ticularize them had been extreame folly, your Wisdomes being so able to direct you, in case God stir your hearts for to take in hand this taske: which if you cheerfully goe through, no doubt but that gale of divine favour, which hath constantly gone along with you, will not now leave you, but bring you to the end. And as your eyes have been blest with many strange sights, and your mouths oftentimes filled, nay strucken dumbe with wonder; so there is no doubt, but if you doe this one thing which now remaines, 30 you shall see the Taper of a learned Piety burne among us, I hope, like an immortall lampe, fed with refined
and

and sublimest knowledge, whilst all those false lights of ignorance, humane forgery, and superstition shall vanish away, or be put out, and the stubborne pervicacy of humane reason turn'd into a gentle compliance to divine truth. You shall see Nature traced through all her Turnings, to a cleare demonstration of her first cause, and every day bring forth varieties of experiments, either to the reliefe, astonishment, or delight of men; you shall then see us freed from all these fabulous illusions and impostures, which have hitherto beset either Traditions or Cures; and Nature which now disguises her selfe into so many shapes, forced into an open veracity and pure nakednesse. You shall see the number of Arts daily increased, and those we knowe already, wonderfully promoted. You shall then see Scheams of Commonwealths brought forth, easie and naturall, and not varied into a multiplicity of crooked *Hypotheses*. You shall then see Policy reconciled to Divinity, Morality, and it self, and yet better able to lay designes and prevent dangers. You will then have it in its native simplicity, and your posterity may at once learne to be both wise and innocent. You shall have the use of the Tongues daily increase, and that judgement of confusion, which hath so long and so heavily laine upon mankinde, by degrees removed. You shall have the wayes of Education made smooth, and your children with a pleasant successe possessed of all the Treasures of reall knowledge, ere they could have thought they had entred the gates. So that when you have added these sights to the former, and witnessed by a happy old age the blessednesse of this Land; you may see the

reines

reines also prosper in the hands of those that shall be your Successours, and melting away in a soft dissolution, finde that Crown above which is owing to fidelity, and that reward below, that the best Law-givers have ever met with; that is, your Names shall increase in the silent motion of Time, and all Posterity shall looke backe upon you, with an eye of Piety and Adoration.

The End.

NOTES

The following notes do not attempt to record all the possible parallels between Hall and such predecessors as Bacon, but enough are given to demonstrate the points made in the Introduction. References to Bacon are to the edition of Spedding, Ellis and Heath, under the title *Works*. Where no specific work is named reference is to the *Advancement of Learning*. References to Milton are to the Bohn edition of the *Prose Works* (*P.W.*).

2. 6–7. The Long Parliament first met 3 November 1640.

2. 15. *great Bugbear of a continuall and shining power.* The House of Lords, which opposed, though ineffectually, the Commons at different stages of the 'first attempt of Free-dome', i.e. the impeachment of Strafford.

2. 25. *one head.* Strafford, executed 12 May 1641.

2. 28–30. The Scottish Army had invaded England during the Second Bishops' War (1640). It continued to occupy the northern counties and was paid £25,000 a month. It remained in England till after the treaty of peace with Scotland (August 1641).

2. 30—**3.** 2. The exact events and people Hall has in mind here are not clear. Most likely he refers to those Parliamentarians who favoured negotiation with Charles, as for instance, in the 'Treaty of Oxford', April 1643. Perhaps also the 'severer Tyranny' refers to Presbyterianism, with the Solemn League and Covenant in mind.

3. 4–12. Again the references are not very clear. The 'Impostume' doubtless refers to the Presbyterian members of Parliament, and the passage as a whole refers to the events leading up to the Self-denying Ordinance of 3 April 1645 and the reform of the army.

3. 12–13. The victories of 1645, especially the Battle of Naseby.

3. 19–24. Hall refers to the situation between the agreement of 26 December 1647 made by Charles and the Scots (the ' Engagement '), and the outbreak of the Second Civil War, when a temporary harmony between Parliament and the Army was achieved. There grew up during this intervening period a considerable Royalist reaction, caused by the general uncertainty and the work of the Scottish Commissioners in London.

3. 25–26. The victories of the Second Civil War, e.g. the Battle of Preston, 17 August 1648.

3. 26—**4.** 6. The reference here is to the various negotiations between Parliament and the King in 1648, especially the ' Treaty of Newport ' (September). The ' concessions ' offered by Charles included the withdrawal of all declarations against Parliament, the acceptance of Presbyterianism for three years, and the handing over of the Army for ten years. The ' former wars ' are the two Civil Wars of 1642–6 and 1647–8.

4. 7–9. Pride's Purge, 6 December 1648.

4. 9–13. The actions are those of the Rump Parliament 1648–9, especially the trial and execution of the King, and the establishment of the Commonwealth.

4. 10. *maleficiate.* Bewitched. *O.E.D.* cites this passage. The word is used in Bacon's *Sylva Sylvarum*, To the reader (Rawley) : ' . . . men's minds, being bound and, as it were, maleficiate by the charms of deceiving notions and theories . . .' (*Works*, ii, 335).

4. 18. *peece of Justice.* The execution of Charles, 30 January 1649.

5. 19–24. Cambridge suffered ejections after the ' Ordinance for regulating the University ' of 22 January 1643/4 ; Oxford's ejections began with the ' Ordinance for the Visitation of the University ' of 1 May 1647.

5. 32—**6.** 5. Hall here perhaps echoes Milton's words on Truth in *Areopagitica* : ' a wicked race of deceivers . . . took the virgin Truth, hewed her lovely form into a thousand pieces, and scattered them to the four winds ' (*P.W.*, ii, 89).

6. 18–24. This is a constantly reiterated argument during the seventeenth century. See R. F. Jones, *Ancients* *and Moderns*, chapter II. The suggestion of the circular theory of progress was given most influential exposition in Hakewill's *Apology of the Power and Providence of God* (1627). The theory had been attacked passim by Bacon, because he thought it made men despair of progress beyond a certain point.

6. 25—**7.** 12. Hall looks back to Bacon who makes the same general point in the *Novum Organum* (*Works*, iv, 114) ; he also parallels Hobbes's view of the ' ill condition, which Man by meer Nature is actually placed in ; though with a possibility to come out of it, consisting partly in the Passions, partly in his Reason '—otherwise the state of nature remains ' solitary, poor, nasty, brutish and short ' (*Leviathan*, Everyman edition, pp. 65, 66). It is possible that Hall saw the *Elements of Law* which had been circulating in manuscript from 1640 and which expresses similar ideas : compare Pt. I, chs. 14–15.

The phrase ' in a direct line ' (**6.** 31) perhaps means ' without memory,' or ' without comparison of one experience with another.'

7. 18–25. Compare Bacon : ' such as were inventors and authors of new arts, endowments, and commodities towards man's life, were ever consecrated amongst the gods themselves ' (*Works*, iii, 301).

8. 1–8. Compare Bacon : ' under learned princes and governors there have been ever the best times : . . . if they be illuminate by learning, they have those notions of religion, policy, and morality, which do preserve them and refrain them from all ruinous and peremptory errors and excesses . . .' (*Works*, iii, 302).

8. 14–18. See Plutarch, life of Pyrrhus (Loeb edition of the *Lives*, ix, 402 ff.).

8. 31. *Plutarch.* The concluding sentences of the life of Epaminondas by Aemylius Probus (i.e. Cornelius Nepos) are much closer to Hall's reference than anything in Plutarch. This life was frequently bound up with Plutarch. The relevant passage is : ' Also in his time he wan to his country by force of armes, the principality of Greece : but after his death his citizens lost it immediatly, and fell daily to decay. . . .

To conclude, before, and after *Epaminondas*, Thebes was vnder foote, and yet commanded all others whiles he stood on his feete ' (North's *Plutarch*, 1631, p. 1126).

9. 16–17. I have failed to discover the reference here.

10. 7. John xxi, 25.

10. '14–17. The historian who most nearly fits this reference, in spite of the obvious discrepancies, is Plutarch : compare the opening paragraphs of his life of Theseus.

10. 20 *either*. Professor Kenneth Muir suggests that this should read *earlier*.

10. 26–30. Compare Bacon : ' We see then how far the monuments of wit and learning are more durable than the monuments of power or of the hands . . . the images of men's wits and knowledges remain in books, exempted from the wrong of time and capable of perpetual renovation ' (*Works*, iii, 318). This whole paragraph of Hall's (pp. 9–10) is close in many points to the penultimate paragraph of Book I of the *Advancement of Learning*.

11. 10. *porismaticall*. ' Following immediately as a corollary.' *O.E.D.* cites this passage for the earliest use of the adjective ; *Horae Vacivae* is cited for the earliest use of the adverb ' porismatically '.

11. 22–24. Compare the quotation (origin not certain) : ' The nature of God is a circle of which the centre is everywhere and the circumference is nowhere ' (*Oxford Dictionary of Quotations*, p. 526).

12. 11–13. Adaptation of 1 Corinthians xiii, 12.

13. 2–3. Psalms 45, 13 and 14.

13. 5–6. Exodus xii, 35–6.

13. 6–7. 2 Chronicles viii, 18.

13. 13–14. This might suggest that Hall is writing before 14 May 1649 when he was promised £100 a year ' for answering pamphlets against the commonwealth ' (*C.S.P.D.*, 1649–50, p. 139 ; quoted Havens, op. cit.).

17. 3. *Litterary*. Learned. Compare **23.** 23.

17. 22–24. Compare Bacon, *Essays*, ' Of Seditions and Troubles ' : ' money is like muck, not good except it be spread ' (*Works*, vi, 410).

18. 21—**19.** 8. This passage is an expansion of the aims of Salomon's House : ' The End of our Foundation is the knowledge of Causes, and secret motions of things ; and the enlarging of the bounds of Human Empire, to the effecting of all things possible ' (Bacon, *New Atlantis, Works*, iii, 156).

19. 14–15. Compare *Areopagitica* : ' a noble and puissant nation rousing herself like a strong man after sleep . . .' *P.W.*, ii, 94).

20. 17–19. See Fable 81 in the Teubner edition of Aesop (*Fabulae Aesopicae Collectae*, 1911).

20. 27. *Positive Law.* Formal, arbitrary law—as opposed to *Natural.*

21. 7–10. A Bill abolishing episcopacy was passed by both Houses 30 January 1643.

22. 29. *brawned.* Made callous.

23. 24–30. Livy xxvi.xi.

23. 32—**24.** 5. This refers especially, no doubt, to the foundation of Leyden University in 1575.

25. 29–32. Compare Milton, *Of Education* : ' we do amiss to spend seven or eight years merely in scraping together so much miserable Latin and Greek, as might be learned otherwise easily and delightfully in one year ' (*P.W.*, iii, 465).

This and the comparisons suggested in the note which follows and in that on **26.** 17 are borrowed from J. B. Mullinger, op. cit., p. 372.

26. 1–3. Compare Milton, op. cit. : ' And for the usual method of teaching arts, I deem it to be an old error of universities . . . that they present their young unmatriculated novices at first coming with the most intellective abstractions of logick and metaphysics ' (*P.W.*, iii, 465–6).

Bacon makes the same complaint about logic and rhetoric : ' scholars in universities come too soon and too unripe to logic and rhetoric ; arts fitter for graduates than children and novices ' (*Works*, iii, 326).

26. 6–7. *as Mounsieur Des-Cartes sayes. Discours de la Méthode*, ed. E. Gilson (1925), p. 70.

26. 17. *Ethicks.* Milton puts Ethics among the final studies when students ' may with some judgement contemplate upon moral good and evil ' (op. cit., *P.W.*, iii, 472).

27. 11 ff. ' We ' here evidently means ' Cambridge.'

28. 16–18. Bacon also bears witness to the learning of the Jesuit colleges (*Works*, iii, 300).

28. 30. *Areopagitick*. First recorded use of word given in *O.E.D.* Perhaps derived from Milton.

30. 9–19. Professor G. H. Turnbull suggests to me that Hall may have been thinking of (1) such foundations as Chelsea College, Gresham College and the Savoy ; (2) such colleges as Eton, Winchester and Dulwich, whose fellowships were regarded by some people at the time as sinecures.

30. 21–2. *that hatefull gagg of licensing*. The Order of Parliament of 14 June 1643 against which *Areopagitica* was directed.

30. 26. *the publicke Library*. It is not quite clear what Hall means here. He may intend a copy to go to each of the university libraries of Oxford and Cambridge ; or he may want the two copies to go to Cambridge, Oxford already having a private arrangement with the Stationers' Company dating from 1610. ' Publicke ' is ' University ' as opposed to ' College.'

31. 6–22. Bacon makes this point—in a less nationalist way—in his demand for ' more intelligence mutual between the universities of Europe than now there is ' (*Works*, iii, 327). The same point is frequently made in the seventeeth century.

33. 29–31. Bacon also makes this distinction (*Works*, iii, 293–4) but deprecates those who ' disperse ' rather than ' augment ' learning. Hall later (**34.** 30 ff.) admits the superiority of the latter.

36. 16–21. Bacon speaks of epitomes as corruptions of history (*Works*, iii, 334).

37. 2–9. Bacon urges the writing of biographies and the ' Narrations and Relations of particular actions ' (*Works*, iii, 338).

38. 20. *Predicaments*. ' The ten categories or classes of predications formed by Aristotle ' (*O.E.D.*).

38. 27–32. Bacon, speaking of the deficiencies in Metaphysics as formerly practised, asserts that ' men (which is the root of all error) have made too untimely a departure and too remote a recess from particulars ' (*Works*, iii, 356).

39. 6 ff. Bacon considers Mathematics ' better laboured and enquired than any of the other forms, which are more immersed into matter ' (*Works*, iii, 359). In the *De Augmentis* he is more aware of defects in Pure Mathematics : in arithmetic, for instance, he complains that there has been no discovery of ' formulas for the abridgment of computation sufficiently various and convenient ' (*Works*, iv, 370)—compare Hall, **40.** 10–19.

40. 11–14. Hall has principally in mind perhaps Oughtred's *Clavis Mathematicae* (1631). Seth Ward introduced this into Cambridge in 1643 as a text-book. Oughtred was also an inventor of mathematical instruments. Hall may have known him through Lilly who intervened to prevent his sequestration in 1645 (*D.N.B.*, xiv, 1250).

41. 2. *Suppute*. Estimate.

41. 19–24. For a list and description of many such books see R. F. Jones, op. cit., especially chapters I–IV.

41. 30—**42.** 1. Compare Bacon (*Works*, iii, 292–3). Bacon specifies ' Gilbertus ' among the moderns—he ' hath made a philosophy out of the observations of a loadstone '.

42. 7–10. Compare Bacon on the evil results of abandoning external matter for scholastic reasoning : ' if [the mind] work upon itself, as the spider worketh his web, then it is endless, and brings forth indeed cobwebs of learning . . . of no substance or profit ' (*Works*, iii, 285–6).

42. 10–27. Compare Bacon, *Novum Organum*, civ : ' The understanding must not however be allowed to jump and fly from particulars to remote axioms . . .' (*Works*, iv, 97).

42. 27–32. This anticipates the *Philosophical Transactions* of the Royal Society. Compare Bacon's ' Catalogue of Particular Histories by Titles ' (*Works*, iv, 265 ff.).

Note on the Text.

The *Humble Motion* exists in one quarto impression. The *Catalogus librorum impressorum* (1843) of the Bodleian records an edition of 1651, but the three copies in the Bodleian are all dated 1649 and are without variants. ' MDCIL ' has doubtless been misread as ' MDCLI.' The present reprint is from the copy in the British Museum and follows this page by page and line by line. The original signatures are not given, but the original pagination is retained. The collation is A-F4 ; the title page [A] and the following blank page [Av] are not included in the pagination ; A2 is page (1). There are few errors in the text. Three turned letters and a few errors of spacing have been silently corrected. Long ſ is replaced by s throughout. The decorations on page (1) are not those of the original. Other changes made in the text are :

5. 17. effectuall] effectualll
6. 24. back] ba ke
10. 21. invincible] invincibie
37. 32. ries, and] ries,, and
44. 15. knowe] knowne